THE ABALONE BOOK

PETER C. HOWORTH

Naturegraph Publishers, Inc., Happy Camp, California 96039

Library of Congress Cataloging in Publication Data

Howorth, Peter, 1944 -
    The abalone book.

    Bibliography: p. 78.
    Includes index.
    1. Abalones.   I. Title.
QL430.5.H34H68   594'.32   78-13204

1988 Update & Printing.

ISBN   0-87961-078-6 Cloth Edition
ISBN   0-87961-077-8 Paper Edition

Naturegraph Publishers, Inc., Happy Camp, California 96039

In memory of Dick Smith

ACKNOWLEDGMENTS

I would like to thank the following members of the California Department of Fish and Game for their help with this book: Captain Howard Martin and Warden Gene Martin for their advice on regulations; biologist Richard Burge for his help with abalone life history; and biologist Dan Miller for his overall critique of the manuscript, particularly abalone - sea otter ecology. I also appreciate the assistance of John Perkins, Cal Marine Associates, and Buzz Owen, Pacific Mariculture, for sharing their intensive knowledge of abalone life history with me. The staff of Ab Lab was also very helpful. Dr. Barry Roth, California Academy of Sciences, deserves thanks for his aid with the paleontological section. Thanks also go to Marjorie Martin for the splendid abalone recipes she provided.

Lawrence Thomas, the Shell Shop, provided access to his rare Florida abalone, for which I am grateful. Mike Wagner, Seafood Specialties, was extremely genial about my frequent intrusions into his commercial abalone processing shop. Thanks also to the Brooks Institute of Photography, and to Rick Terry and Dorothy Lawson, two outstanding photographers whose work strengthened this book. Special thanks go to Roy Hattori for permitting me to use his outstanding photograph of abalone diving in the old days.

Special thanks also go to my mother, for her proofreading; to my wife Jane, for typing the manuscript and making all the drawings in this text; to Sevrin Housen for his careful and constructive editing; and to everyone who, knowingly or not, helped me gather this material.

CONTENTS

INTRODUCTION

Many people marvel at the iridescent swirls gracing the interior of an abalone shell; others exclaim that their first bite of an abalone steak reminds them more of Wiener schnitzel than of seafood. Yet seldom do people realize what causes the lovely colors in the shell, or that this animal is really a huge, flattened snail.

This book stems from several years of research. A scantling of the contents evolved from digging among the meager stack of scientific papers written on abalones. But the bulk of this material was gleaned the hard way: from observing the animals in their undersea habitat, and from prying open the lips of the recalcitrant few who actually knew something about abalones.

The text is divided into five parts. The first section relates the evolution of this resource, beginning with the fossil records and followed by man's intervention into the fragile food web which had been woven around the abalone. The next part outlines the problems currently plaguing the resource and introduces some possible solutions. Following this is a section on abalone life history, then another on the eight species of American abalones. The last part deals with cleaning and preparing abalones, including traditional and innovative recipes as well as tips for shell collectors. Appendixes highlight the information, and a detailed, cross-referenced index is provided for easy access to the text.

It is hoped that this book will foster a better understanding of American abalones. Only through education can we learn to live with our fellow creatures rather than upon them.

Haliotis lomaënsis This half-inch-long (1.3 cm) fossil abalone from the Upper Cretaceous Period resembles the black abalone of today. It was found at Point Loma, California, and is approximately eighty million years old. *(Photo by Peter C. Howorth; courtesy California Academy of Sciences, San Francisco)*

Haliotis elsmerensis An ancestor to the red abalone, this fossil abalone is three inches (about 76 mm) in length and approximately twenty-five million years old. *(Photo by Peter C. Howorth; courtesy California Academy of Sciences, San Francisco)*

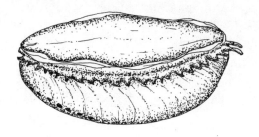

PART I

EVOLUTION OF THE ABALONE RESOURCE

PREHISTORIC EVIDENCE

By the time the last dinosaur had disappeared from the earth, *Haliotis lomaënsis*, the ancestor of today's black abalone, had evolved. *H. lomaënsis* lived during the Upper Cretaceous Period in the vicinity of what is now Point Loma, California. About eighty million years old, this half-inch (1.3 cm) fossil is the oldest known abalone species in the world and, interestingly enough, differs little from its modern counterpart.

Some seven to twenty-five million years ago, a number of other forms evolved in California that resemble several species existing today.* During the Miocene Epoch, marine algae abounded and probably were used as food by abalones. Sea urchins also existed then, and it is likely that they competed with abalones for sustenance. Probably the earliest abalone predators were fishes, crustaceans and certain mollusks (cephalopods). Although the bulk of the west coast

---

* *H. elsmerensis* is similar to *H. rufescens*; *H. lasis* looks like *H. fulgens*; *H. palaea* resembles *H. corrugata*; and *H. koticki* is close to *H. k. assimilis* in appearance.

abalone population apparently evolved in California, some species spread south into Baja California, while others ranged widely northward, one as far as the Aleutian Islands west of Alaska.

The abalone survived through the years with little change. The flattened, shieldlike shell withstood countless predators, although in recent geologic time the abalone's survival was threatened by the sea otter.

Unlike its predecessors, the sea otter was cunning enough to use tools to remove the abalone from its ocean stronghold. Using stones to break the convex shells, this animal preyed upon the abalone in a way no other organism had. Only a few creatures, such as great white sharks and bald eagles, preyed in turn upon otters, at least until man arrived.

When prehistoric man came to the west coast is unknown, but it was rather recently. Inevitably he took to the sea for food, foraging first for intertidal shellfish, then for larger organisms found offshore, including the sea otter.

Early man congregated near sources of food and water. Even today, much evidence remains of these cultures. In their kitchen middens are innumerable empty clam, mussel and abalone shells which once had yielded food.

The empty shells were very important for utensils, such as bowls, for fishhooks, wood scrapers, ornamental beads, necklaces, and decorations on tools and utensils. They were even used for bartering with inland tribal groups. Some abalone shell artifacts have been found thousands of miles from the west coast.

When native Americans first began to prey on abalones and otters is unknown, although it certainly was within the last several thousand years. These early people lived in relative harmony with nature, thriving on the abundant natural resources.

A NATURAL FOOD WEB

A group of interrelated organisms, which relies directly or indirectly upon one another for food, forms what is called a food web.

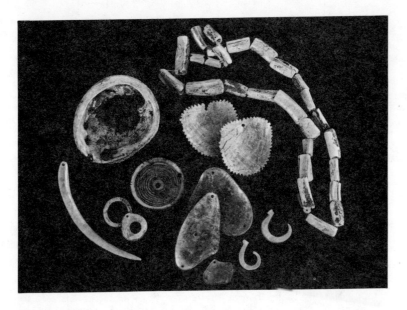

ABALONE SHELL ARTIFACTS   Abalone shells were used for many purposes by the Pacific coast Indians; artifacts shown here are necklace, pendants, bowl and fishhooks. *(Photo by Dorothy Lawson, Brooks Institute; courtesy Santa Barbara Museum of Natural History)*

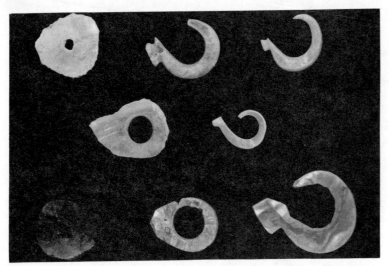

ABALONE FISHHOOKS   Four examples on left show the evolution of an abalone shell into a fishhook. Examples on right are of fishhooks used by Pacific coast Indians. *(Photo by Dorothy Lawson, Brooks Institute; courtesy Santa Barbara Museum of Natural History)*

Each organism is dependent upon many others for its existence. The primary elements in the abalone food web are sunshine and raw materials: nutrients for sustaining vast algae beds blanketing coastal waters. These algae photosynthesize organic compounds for their own nourishment, releasing oxygen as a by-product. The oxygen is utilized by marine animals in respiration.

Algae serve as fodder for grazing marine animals such as sea urchins and abalones. Sea urchins are voracious algae feeders that move in fronts toward food sources. Abalones are more sedentary and rely upon a steady food supply.

Preying upon abalones and sea urchins are a variety of creatures, including fishes, crabs, echinoderms and even other mollusks, such as octopi. Yet the main abalone predator is the sea otter. It is able to eat the equivalent of one-fourth of its body weight daily. This amounts to over twenty pounds for a large male.

The native Americans kept population levels of sea otters and littoral abalone beds in check. Offshore beds were, and still are, controlled by foraging marine predators, but probably at no time was the ecological balance within this food web more stable than it was a few centuries ago.

EUROPEAN IMPACT ON THE FOOD WEB

When an essential strand in any web is destroyed or damaged, the entire web is affected. The more intense the damage, the more intense the effect. In the 1700 s and 1800 s fur was a prized commodity in Europe and Asia, and the sea otter bore the finest fur of all. Inevitably, they were slaughtered for their precious pelts. By the turn of this century, the sea otter was dangerously close to extinction. Eleventh-hour legislation undoubtedly saved this animal.

The advent of "civilized" man did more than nearly exterminate the otter. It also devastated the cultures of native Americans, through treacherous greed, disease and even religion. Gone forever was a way of life which had taken thousands of years to evolve.

Shorn of natural predators, abalones and sea urchins multiplied

SIMPLIFIED FOOD WEB: sunlight, kelp, abalones, sea urchins, sheephead,
sea otter, man

at an ever-increasing rate, soon dominating shallow underwater zones. Urchins devoured entire kelp forests, followed, to a lesser degree, by abalones.

Dense shellfish populations developed, and resultant mass fertilizations caused many seedling abalones to settle into areas where they previously had not existed. Within a few decades, abalones covered many areas of ocean bottom two and three animals deep. (It is still this way in some unharvested sections of northern California.) This was an unnatural condition in which the overall quality of these populations undoubtedly suffered from extensive food competition. Crowded for living space, they grew thick, high shells, rather than the flat, thin shells associated with fast-growing, healthy specimens.

CROWDED ABALONES   These black abalones, jammed into a crevice, compete vigorously for food.   Eroded shells are typical of such populations. *(Photo by Peter C. Howorth)*

A NEW FISHERY IS CREATED

While abalone populations continued to increase unchecked, thousands of Chinese immigrated to California following the Gold Rush. The abalone, a great Asian delicacy, was a real bonanza for the Chinese. In Baja and southern California, including the offshore islands, Asians began harvesting the incredibly dense beds of intertidal abalones. As stocks of black and green abalones were depleted, the fishermen moved north to San Luis Obispo County.

The industrious Chinese were successful harvesters and, by 1879, had annual catches in excess of four million pounds. In 1900, however, county ordinances were passed that made it illegal to gather abalones from less than twenty feet of water. These measures were highly discriminatory since only Asians and a few surviving Native Americans ate abalones at that time. The regulations completely halted their commercial abalone operations.

Undaunted by the new regulations, Japanese fishermen began diving for abalones. These hardy people utilized old rice wine casks as floats to rest on after each dive. They would take a few deep breaths, dive to the bottom and return to the surface with their catch. They quickly earned the nickname of "Saké barrel divers" because of their unusual technique.

Saké barrel diving was not a very efficient method since divers had to spend considerable time on the surface getting their breath and warming up between dives. New diving equipment and personnel arrived from their homeland, however, and for many years helmeted Japanese divers plodded across the ocean bottom from Monterey to Morro Bay. Even their boats, a few of which survive today, came from Japan.

These early abalone boats were sculled with a long oar at the transom. While the diver picked, a man continually worked a manual pump that supplied the diver with air. Another crewman tended the diving hose, whereas a fifth cut kelp away from the floating air hose with a long-handled, hooked kelp knife.

Some say Japanese fishermen secretly harvested sea otters, sending them to Japan on ships which visited our coast prior to World

War II. If this were true, the otter pelts would not only have provided divers with added income, but also would have kept in check the divers' main competitors for abalones.

These wily fishermen completely monopolized the commercial abalone field in California until 1929, when abalones really began to gain popularity as a domestic product.

A commercial fishery was also started in British Columbia as early as 1913, in which pinto abalones were picked intertidally, processed and canned by enterprising Canadians. The operation was far from extensive, however, and a few hundred cases of canned abalones were considered an exceptional yearly harvest.

JAPANESE DIVER   Commercial abalone diver Roy Hattori is assisted by tenders as he prepares for a dive off Monterey, California. This was a common sight in the 'twenties and 'thirties. *(Photo courtesy of Roy Hattori)*

A CALIFORNIA DELICACY EMERGES

Early Spanish settlers, together with the Mexican people who followed, regarded abalones as poisonous. When they first arrived in California, these people had scornfully ignored the Indians' warnings regarding shellfish. The native Americans knew that mussels were toxic to humans at certain times of the year.* As filter feeders, mussels ingest poisonous microorganisms that accumulate in lethal dosages within their tissues. Since mussels were a popular European food item, the Spaniards devoured California mussels with great enthusiasm, not realizing their danger. A number of settlers died from shellfish poisoning, which perhaps explains why others refused to eat abalones. Had they listened to warnings, they would have been able to eat mussels *and* abalones. Abalones are perfectly safe to eat year-round because they are algae grazers, not filter feeders.

Around 1900, a small restaurant opened on the main street of old Monterey. "Pop" Ernest Doelter, an experienced cook, soon developed an unusual item on his menu: abalones. His recipe is still followed (see RECIPES).

His unique product gained considerable notoriety, and by 1913 he was preparing it for the better San Francisco restaurants. In 1915, at the Panama Pacific International Exposition, "Pop" introduced his epicurean specialty to people from all over the world. His fame assured, he returned to Monterey after World War I and opened another restaurant on Fisherman's Wharf, where he continued to serve his specialty until his death in 1935. Doelter was the first to develop the abalone as a domestic gourmet food item.

With increasing demands for this resource, American entrepreneurs attempted to corner the commercial abalone diving field, but the Japanese kept their trade secrets to themselves. With the advent of World War II, however, all people of Japanese descent, even American-born citizens of Asian ancestry, were removed to "relocation centers." These were nothing more than concentration camps for the

---

* May through October are the quarantine months, although it is wise to check wth health authorities before eating mussels, since occasionally they are poisonous at other times.

hapless Nesei. Most of these unfortunate people found themselves out of business after the war, with Caucasians at the helms of their abalone boats.

In British Columbia, a few small abalone canneries still operated, although commercial production was nil compared to the California fishery.

ABALONE PROCESSORS AT WORK   Abalones at commercial processing plants are first removed from shells, then trimmed, sliced and pounded. *(Photo by Peter C. Howorth; courtesy Seafood Specialties, Santa Barbara)*

PRESENT STATUS OF COMMERCIAL FISHERY

In California, although many commercial abalone permits are re-
newed each year, less than fifty divers actually make a living from abalones. Competition is intense, with considerable pressure upon the few
areas still open to commercial divers. A small fishery exists precariously
along a short stretch near Half Moon Bay. From there, divers occasionally venture out to the distant Farallon Islands, a rather dangerous area
to work, since the water is cold, rough and frequently visited by great
white sharks.

By the early 1980s, sea otters had destroyed the commercial
and sport fisheries from Santa Cruz to Point Sal, south of Pismo Beach
(see Pressure From Sea Otters). At Purisima Point, off Vandenberg Air
Force Base, is one of the last great red abalone beds in southern
California. From there to Carpinteria, a viable commercial fishery
exists. Several processing shops service this abalone fleet. Various
sections of Santa Barbara County's coast are "dead," meaning no
commercial quantities of abalones are present, but extensive abalone
beds still thrive in some areas.

Offshore are the four Santa Barbara Channel Islands: Anacapa,
Santa Cruz, Santa Rosa and San Miguel. They are heavily fished by
commercial divers, since protected anchorages exist for nearly any
weather condition. Also, the water is consistently clear, providing
good working conditions. Moreover, outer islands receive comparatively little sport diving pressure.

Although Anacapa and Santa Barbara Islands once comprised
the Channel Islands National Monument, administered by the National
Park Service, the water surrounding these islands belongs to
California. The National Park Service's jurisdiction was overthrown by
a 1978 Supreme Court decision which gave control of the water back
to the state. Several areas closed by previous federal action are now
open, although impending legislation may close parts of Anacapa and
Santa Barbara Islands to commercial abalone harvesting. The four
northern Channel Islands and Santa Barbara Island are now part of
Channel Islands National Park.

Farther out is San Nicolas Island. This island receives less pressure because of its remoteness, with rough weather and a lack of decent anchorages keeping most divers away. Furthermore, certain sections of San Nicolas are closed periodically by the military.

Some boats work out of Los Angeles, Long Beach and Newport Beach. They fish the outer islands, the ocean side of Santa Catalina—the channel side is closed to commercial divers—and San Clemente Island to the south. These boats occasionally travel to Cortez Bank, a shallow spot some eightly miles offshore from San Diego. A small fishery also is based in San Diego. Divers fish a short stretch of mainland coast, San Clemente Island and Cortez Bank.

Many boats work out of Los Angeles, Long Beach and Newport Beach. They fish the outer islands, the ocean side of Santa Catalina—the channel side is closed to commercial divers—and San Clemente Island to the south. These boats occasionally travel to Cortez Bank, a shallow spot some eighty miles offshore from San Diego. A small fishery also is based in San Diego. Divers fish a short stretch of mainland coast, San Clemente Island and Cortez Bank.

MODERN ABALONE BOAT AND GEAR   Abalone boats are built ruggedly, designed to carry heavy loads. The abalones are stowed on deck and covered with wet burlap. Air compressor supplies diver with air through long hose. *(Photo by Peter C. Howorth)*

Most abalone boats are twenty to thirty feet long. Many are equipped with live wells to keep abalones alive for extended periods. The boats are open, with large, raised wash decks and tiny doghouse cabins that provide only minimal accommodations. Built with no frills, they are simply working platforms that convey divers to and from the fishing grounds. Most are propelled by gasoline inboard - outboard engines. They are designed to plane heavy loads in moderate seas.

Diving equipment consists of a surface air compressor and volume tank, a diving hose—usually about three hundred feet long—and the second stage of a scuba regulator, which has a mouthpiece for breathing. The hose is attached to the diver's weight belt. Most divers wear a wetsuit, swim fins, a conventional face mask and gloves. They carry a net bag large enough to hold a few dozen abalones, and an abalone iron, called a "bottom bar," which is fitted with tines representing the legal sizes for each abalone species. Divers measure abalones with the abalone iron before removing them.

COMMERCIAL ABALONE IRON

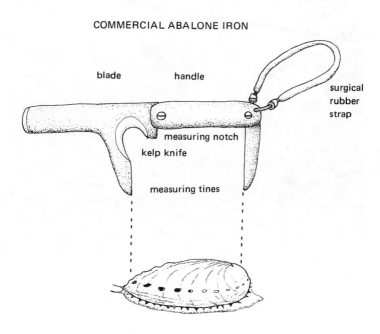

blade   handle

surgical rubber strap

measuring notch

kelp knife

measuring tines

The modus operandi varies from crew to crew, but generally the fishermen will either tie the boat to kelp or anchor it at the diving grounds. One or two divers then systematically cover the bottom for abalones. Most divers have their tender watch the boat, operate the air compressor, tend hose and lift baskets. A few divers operate solo, with no one aboard while they are below.

PICKING ABALONES UNDER WATER   Commercial diver Bob McMillen harvests abalones thirty feet down. *(Photo by Peter C. Howorth)*

Each diver works as quickly as possible. When his basket is comfortably full, he returns it to the boat or snaps it to a weighted line under the boat. Abalones are double-checked for legal size by the tender, then counted, stacked on deck or stowed in live wells. They will generally keep two or three days if the first layer is placed shell down and subsequent layers are placed shell up. This way the shells protect the animals from the hot deck and sun. Wet burlap is usually dropped over deckloads of abalones to keep them cool.

After an area is worked out, the boat moves on until the diver either gets tired or runs out of time. In deep water, bottom time must be limited to avoid the bends. In shallow water, however, divers are able to stay down for hours. Some divers make twenty or thirty "jumps" (dives) a day, working from six to ten hours under water, although the average is probably only three to six hours.

A few boats work "live," the boat following the diver around wherever he goes. Although the diver does not have to return to the boat with each basket, this method places added demands upon the crew and increases overhead with the engine running all day. Some crews "drift boat," the diver simply following the direction the boat is drifting as he works. This is quite efficient in deep water where little kelp is present. After one to five days, depending on the weather and the method of stowing abalones, the boats return to port and unload their catch.

Once abalones are unloaded from the boats, they are trucked to nearby processing shops where they are shucked, gutted, skinned, sliced and pounded. Divers are paid by the processed pound. They usually figure prices in dozens for easy reference. Red abalones, which yield the most poundage, brought up to two hundred dollars a dozen in the 1980s, while the smaller pinks, whites and greens brought less than a hundred dollars a dozen and blacks only fifteen to twenty dollars a dozen. Other species, including pinto and threaded abalones, were occasionally processed and ran from twelve to eighteen dollars a dozen. (In 1985, the cost of top quality abalones was some twenty dollars a pound in retail fish markets, an expensive luxury.)

Divers are fortunate to work twelve to fifteen days a month during the ten-month season. Bad weather, equipment breakdowns and crew fatigue make commercial abalone diving a very demanding profession. Few divers last long because of excessive physical demands.

California lobster fishermen can harvest black abalones for bait throughout the six-month lobster season. They pick black abalones on shore during low tides at the islands. Some lobster fishermen run hundreds of traps that must be baited every two days. Because one to three whole black abalones are used in each trap, the number used is considerable.

Since the late 1960s, commercial divers have been exploiting the pinto abalone beds of British Columbia and Alaska. In Alaska the flurry has been brief and inconclusive, for the water there is bitterly cold and often extremely rough. It may only be a matter of time before Alaska develops a commerical abalone fishery because abalones are certainly there for the taking.

British Columbia already has a thriving abalone fishery. With the advent of skin diving came a new breed of Canadian fisherman: the commercial abalone diver. In 1976, divers landed over six hundred thousand pounds of abalones. Whereas California's catches dwindled, British Columbia's production boomed.

The Canadians mainly fish the east side of the Queen Charlotte Islands and along the mainland coast nearby. Abalones are frozen whole aboard the boats or kept in floating receivers until the fishermen return to port. There, catches are usually sold whole to the highest bidder.

In Washington and Oregon, commercial abalone diving is prohibited.

PRESENT STATUS OF SPORT FISHERY

Aside from a few hardy adventurers, nearly all sport pickers before World War II collected abalones on shore during low tides. From Alaska to northern California shore picking still continues, although skin diving for abalones is now favored by most sportsmen.

In Alaska and British Columbia, shore pickers and divers harvest pinto abalones in semiprotected stretches of the Inland Passage during spells of good weather. Pintos are picked by skin divers in the San Juan Islands of Washington, while Oregon sportsmen harvest red abalones from Coos Bay to the California border. Although other species are found throughout Oregon, only the red is taken because the size limit on all Oregon abalones is eight inches (23 cm.). This automatically precludes the smaller species.

From northern California to Santa Cruz are large quantities of red abalones for shore pickers and divers alike. Some areas boast abalones stacked two and three deep (see European Impact On The Food Chain). Other areas, particularly those readily accessible to the public, are not so productive.

Considerable portions of the coast in northern California are inaccessible, at least by land. High cliffs plummeting straight into the sea dominate many areas. Other spots are on private property. Still, pickers take many abalones from the north coast. With the boating boom, formerly inaccessible areas are now being fished from small craft.

Weather is another problem along the north coast. Breakers and strong winds often make the sea treacherous. Cold, dirty water is also a detriment to sport diving.

Although offshore beds from Santa Cruz to Point Sal had been decimated by sea otters by the 1980s, a few crevice-protected abalones may still be gleaned from the littoral zone within the otters' range (see Pressure From Sea Otters).

The area immediately above Point Conception (Jalama Beach County Park) to the Mexican border is largely accessible by land or sea. The water is usually fairly warm, clear and calm, and divers can harvest abalones nearly any time.

Diving is fair from Point Conception to Carpinteria. A large "blank" spot runs from above Ventura to the Ventura - Los Angeles County line. This area is covered with sand and therefore uninhabitable for abalones. A few abalones may be found from Point Mugu to above Malibu.   Santa Monica is closed to fishing because of sewage pollution.

Extensive pollution, disturbed habitats and sandy stretches account for much of the coast from Malibu to Newport Beach, with the exception of Palos Verdes Peninsula. From Newport Beach, abalone beds extend sporadically to the Mexican border, although much of this coastline is closed due to military activities.

At the offshore islands, Catalina is first in popularity and Anacapa second. Santa Cruz Island is a favorite of sportsmen from Santa Barbara, Ventura and Oxnard. Santa Rosa Island is seldom heavily dived except during lobster season. San Miguel, Santa Barbara, San Nicolas and San Clemente are even less popular because these islands are far offshore and the sea around them is often quite rough. Cortez Bank, some eighty miles off San Diego, is seldom visited by sport divers.

In California, skin and scuba divers are allowed to pick abalones from Yankee Point, in Monterey County, south to the Mexican border. Only skin diving and shore picking are allowed north of this point. Sportsmen are limited to four abalones per person per day in California, three in Oregon, five in Washington, twelve in British Columbia and fifty in Alaska. The "abs" are usually kept in "goodie bags" until the diver returns to shore.

Shore pickers are a hardy set who venture forth in gray, early morning hours to catch low tides. The lower the tide, the better the picking, since more intertidal area is exposed. Wetsuits, waders, rubber boots and even swim suits with tennis shoes are their favorite garb.

Shore pickers often dot beaches like ants, their equipment consisting merely of abalone irons and gunny sacks. Remote areas studded with algae-covered rocks are the best hunting grounds.

Either way the abalone is picked, it is a sport demanding considerable stamina, experience and luck. The rewards are well worth the trouble, however, for west coast abalones are the best eating and largest in the world.

SHORE PICKING ABALONES   This sportsman is gathering black abalones in the intertidal region. Shore foraging for abalones is popular in Northern California and certain parts of the Pacific Northwest. *(Photo by Peter C. Howorth)*

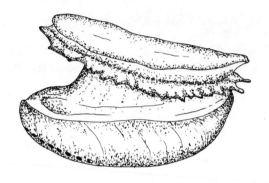

PART II

PROBLEMS WITH THE ABALONE RESOURCE

POLLUTION

During the 1930 s and 1940 s, thousands of people moved to California. With these hordes came all the problems inherent with a mass encroachment. Food demands increased, and with this, the demand for abalones. Divers soon were stripping the excess of abalones that had been left untouched since the sea otter's reign.

With the population boom came other problems. Major south coast areas oozed millions of gallons of sewage into the sea, ultimately destroying many habitats. Most animals were unable to tolerate this. A few creatures, such as sea urchins, were able to utilize sewage as food, even though detritus from sewage actually blocked out life-giving sunlight as it settled. Countless young algae plants were slowly smothered by this sewage and were eaten by foraging urchins. Kelp beds, which provided shelter and food for many creatures including abalones, were thus destroyed. Certainly many other organisms in vulnerable juvenile stages of development perished also.

COMMERCIAL PRESSURE

As each abalone species grew scarcer in California, less desirable ones were exploited. What appeared to be a relatively stable fishery was actually one which kept expanding to maintain consistent productivity. Red abalones were first to be heavily exploited, followed by pinks, greens, and blacks. Today whites (Sorensens) and even diminutive threaded abalones are being harvested commercially.

In 1971, a law was passed by the California State Legislature legalizing the exportation of abalones out of the state and country, thus opening an outside market for a state resource. Soon black abalones, too difficult to process conventionally for domestic consumption, were being shipped to Asia in frozen bulk packages. There they were thawed and processed in other ways by the Asians.

Universally heavy pressure has been placed upon commercial abalone beds for some thirty years. Federal and state closures, coupled with intensive sport diving pressure in southern California, have squeezed the commercial fishery to the offshore islands and to the coast north of Carpinteria, California.

Oregon and Washington fishery experts, realizing that their abalone beds would not last under commercial pressure, simply prohibited commercial abalone diving, neatly solving the problem before it was even created.

In British Columbia and Alaska, cold, rough water proved to be the most effective detriment to overexploitation. Still, authorities are ever-watchful over their resources. Hopefully, they will realistically and swiftly deal with any problems that arise.

PRESSURE FROM SEA OTTERS

Following World War II, sea otters in California proliferated, soon spreading from their original Point Sur habitat to Santa Cruz in the north and Avila in the south. In their wake remained only a few tough-shelled, small invertebrates. Every large, exposed, edible invertebrate within their diving range was essentially wiped out, including the abalone. This is no exaggeration. A transect survey was made at

Cayucos, a productive region for red abalones for over forty years. The survey was done on a private ranch, inaccessible to sport divers and closed to commercial divers because of the shallow water law. An area of one hundred square meters was minutely examined. Divers found over two red abalones per square meter, or approximately two hundred thirty red abalones in the area. They surveyed the same area three years later, after otters had gone through, and found virtually *no* living abalones—only a few empty shells broken by otters.

Unfortunately sea otters eat nearly all shellfish, including juveniles. This eventually cripples invertebrate breeding populations, hence the "deserts" left by otters. Crustaceans, including edible-sized crabs; mollusks, primarily abalones, large top shells and Pismo clams; echino-

SEA OTTER DINES ON ABALONE IN CENTRAL CALIFORNIA COASTAL WATERS *(Photo by Ernest H. Brooks II, Brooks Institute)*

derms, particularly urchins—have all been practically exterminated within the otters' range. But a few animals, protected by deep crevices and immovable boulders, have survived. Only algae forests, containing a few starfishes, small mollusks and tiny crustaceans, remain within the otters' range.

The commercial abalone industry of Morro Bay, which was the capital of the red abalone business for thirty years, is now at a standstill. In 1966, over one hundred boats operated out of this port. Today, those that still operate come out of Santa Barbara and ports farther south.

SPORT FISHERY PRESSURE

California Fish and Game statistics indicate that sport catches equal or exceed commercial abalone landings. While the commercial fishery is limited to a short stretch of coast and to a few offshore islands, the sport fishery extends from border to border, except for a few areas that are either inaccessible or closed by federal or state government. Sport divers and shore pickers, numbering in the thousands, do place considerable pressure upon remaining abalone beds.

In Oregon, Washington, British Columbia and Alaska, far less stress is felt upon the resource. Not only are fewer people involved, but also fewer abalones, at least in numbers of species. Moreover, the cold, frequently rough water halts all but the most stalwart foragers. No major problem seems to exist from sport fishery pressure north of California at this time.

MISUSE OF THE RESOURCE

Like many of our precious resources, little importance was attached at first to abalones. Favored by Native Americans and later by Asians, the exploitation of this excellent shellfish went unheralded for decades. Only when the abalone became an important domestic source of food and income were any significant protective measures forthcoming. Although legislation did serve as a stopgap to certain critical problems, measures were only initiated after the problems had become critical. Typically enough, this occurred long before biologists had conducted any serious work in the field. It was not until 1948 that the California Department of Fish and Game published its first biological paper on abalones: *The Abalones of California,* by Paul Bonnot. This was nearly one hundred years after the Chinese began their commercial harvesting.

As the industry gained in economic importance, revenue became available for research. Fish and Game biologists made several studies over the years resulting in some essential changes in regulations.

The most important regulation is unquestionably the size limit for each abalone species. Without a minimum size limit, breeding populations would be wiped out, resulting in the virtual elimination of an important resource. Morro Bay, its sub-legal abalones decimated by sea otters, is a good example of what can happen when breeding populations are removed.

Unfortunately, a small percentage of sportsmen and commercial abalone divers also take "shorts" (illegal-size abalones). But most people are reasonably conscientious and observe size limits. Fines with possible jail terms serve as detriments to would-be offenders.

Probably the second most serious misuse of the resource comes from improper picking methods. This begins long before the diver (or shore picker) sets out for abalones. Many neophytes, and even some experienced divers, can only recognize abalones by shell characteristics. Since shells are frequently festooned with marine encrustations, it is essential to be able to recognize each species by characteristics of the animal (see PART IV).

PROPER METHOD OF PICKING ABALONES

Abalones are legally in season several months out of the year. Number limits are generous, providing each sportsman with enough food for several meals and each commercial diver with a decent income.

Picking an abalone before it is identified is a mistake; each abalone should be identified and measured before it is removed. If this is impossible, remove the largest abalone in the group and measure it first. If it is short, leave the others alone. By law, each short must be immediately replaced on the rock from which it was taken. When you replace a short, be certain it is firmly clamped down. Loose abalones are extremely vulnerable to predators.

Use a legal abalone iron for prying off abalones. This flat metal bar is approximately a foot long with various indicators for each legal size. (Size specifications are given in Fish and Game regulations, available free at most sporting goods stores.) Extreme care must be taken to avoid cutting each abalone when removing it. A wounded abalone, even when returned to the rock, often will die from its wounds or become too weak to hold on. No coagulative elements are present in abalone blood, so even a minor wound can be fatal. Once injured, an abalone is easy prey for several voracious predators found throughout California. Experienced pickers seldom even scratch an abalone. They favor rocks with the iron and not the abalone; if the iron is always scraping rocks, the abalone will not be damaged.

SPORT ABALONE IRON

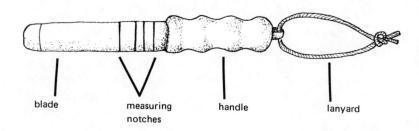

blade   measuring   handle   lanyard
               notches

SOLUTIONS TO PROBLEMS

Current Fish and Game regulations reflect years of hard-learned lessons. Keep well versed on them, for they are frequently revised as new problems develop.

A great deal can be done by individuals. We should fight to stop pollution by those who are using the Pacific Ocean as a cesspool. Projects are frequently underway for cleaning up our environment, including our ocean, and these projects deserve full support.

Mariculture—the artificial raising of marine organisms in controlled environments—certainly holds some promise for the future. Several organizations have tried to grow abalones in tanks to commercially profitable size. The main obstacle thus far has been the slow growing cycle of abalones. It takes them years to reach harvestable size because each abalone requires considerable space and water while growing. To maintain such an abalone stock is very expensive; a single mistake can ruin years of careful work.

One solution is to raise them only to juvenile size, then plant them on the ocean floor. Unfortunately, this would require transplanting huge quantities before substantial gains could be expected.

Another, perhaps more viable solution, is to place juveniles into receivers which can be periodically jammed with algae to feed the abalones. Experiments conducted by Cal Marine Associates, a mariculture firm in Cayucos, California, have shown this to be feasible, at least for commercial growing.

As for replenishing diminished wild stocks, a joint project between the California Department of Fish and Game and the University of California's Sea Grant Program should determine if this is feasible. If it can be done, increased funds and intensified action may provide a beginning for enhancing the abalone resource in the 1980s.

The real future of the resource remains with the public, particularly with the individual. Remember to take only what you can use so there will be abalones next time.

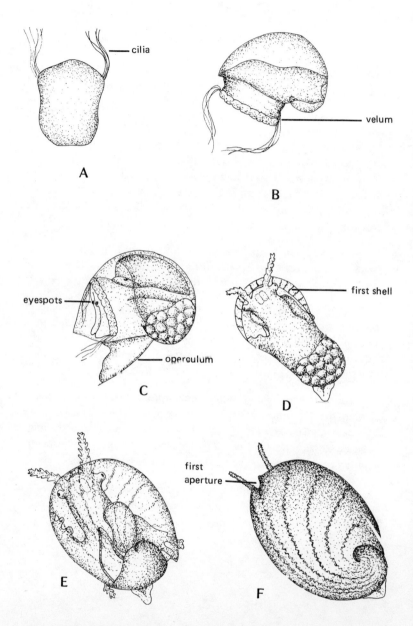

ABALONE GROWTH STAGES A) Trochophore larva after hatching; B) Veliger with velum; C) Veliger with operculum and eyespots; D) First shell forming (post larval); E) Shell developing into beginning of juvenile form; F) First aperture forming in shell.

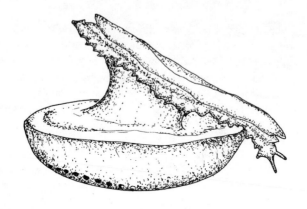

PART III

ABALONE LIFE HISTORY

REPRODUCTION AND GROWTH

Abalones seem to spawn most often during late spring and summer. Triggered by a number of factors, such as a shift to warmer water, male abalones release whitish clouds of gametes through their apertures. Females usually release ova after males spawn, although the presence of sperm may not be the main factor influencing them. Generally, abalones lift up their shells, then move them forcefully up and down a few times while releasing sex products into the water.

Population densities directly influence the success of each spawning. If abalones are few and far between, chances of a successful fertilization are slight. The physiological condition of the breeding stock is also an important factor. Abalones weakened by parasites or wounds may not be capable of producing viable gametes. Extensive grazing by other abalones or sea urchins may leave an abalone weakened by hunger and temporarily unable to breed. Sexual activity seems to be minimal during periods of rapid shell growth, since presumably much energy is expended then.

Once an egg is fertilized, development is swift. In less than an hour the egg usually divides, and in less than a day a tiny swimming larva appears. This free-swimming ciliated larva, called a trochophore, soon develops a structure known as the velum, an umbrellalike appendage which allows the animal to swim. Some authorities believe that this ciliated structure also traps plankton for food, although abalones have been raised in sterilized, filtered sea water to advanced stages without appreciable loss.

Within a day or so, the creature develops into a free-swimming form with a tiny shell called a veliger. By the second day, an operculum appears; this is a hatchlike structure used to close the shell entrance. By the following day, the foot is usually developed, enabling the animal to crawl as well as to swim.

In less than a week, the abalone settles to the bottom and quickly hides in dark, protected areas comparatively safe from predators. The creature then begins to eat diatoms with its rapidly developing radula, a rasplike tongue characteristic of snails. By the end of the first week, the minute crawler, smaller than a sand grain, loses its velum and the shell begins to grow in a different shape. The operculum disappears.

Soon the first notch is formed in the shell, then the first respiratory pore. By this time, most metamorphic fatalities have occurred. The entire process, from egg to juvenile, takes place in just a few weeks. Precise times of each metamorphic change vary. Most abalones reach legal size at five to ten years of age; a few may live to be fifty years old.

The diet of emerging juveniles soon switches from diatoms to coralline algae. Larger algae, such as giant kelp, are eaten by adult abalones.

THE ABALONE SHELL

Like many juvenile forms, young abalones are thin, colorful and very agile compared to adults. Their delicate shells are often multicolored, ornamented with oblique color bands on the margins together with streaks or chevron markings on the flat shell surfaces. Some specimens exhibit spiral banding which may continue into the adult form. All *these* color patterns are the result of genetic factors. Quite likely, mottled colors of small shells serve as camouflage, breaking up regular outlines. These colors are seldom seen under water, since sunlight is filtered out by the density of the water.

Concentric color bands are the result of dietary fluctuations. These bands follow the growing edge of the shell. The outside of the shell is covered with periostracum, a translucent, shellaclike covering which protects the shell from various encrusting organisms.

THE ABALONE SHELL   (outside parts)

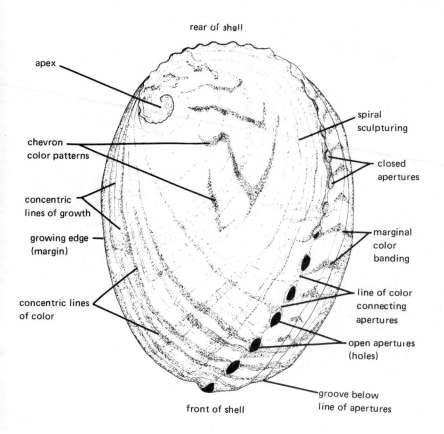

rear of shell

apex

chevron
color patterns

concentric
lines of growth

growing edge
(margin)

concentric lines
of color

spiral
sculpturing

closed
apertures

marginal
color
banding

line of color
connecting
apertures

open apertures
(holes)

groove below
line of apertures

front of shell

Underneath is a pigmented, heavy layer followed by a pearly, nacreous inner layer. The calcium carbonate shell is formed by a structure called the mantle.

Contrary to prior literature, all Pacific coast abalones can develop either a muscle scar or a concentration of nacreous clumps where the muscle was attached to the shell. This usually occurs in older adults. Fast-growing shells frequently develop little or no scars until they are quite large.

THE ABALONE SHELL   (inside parts)

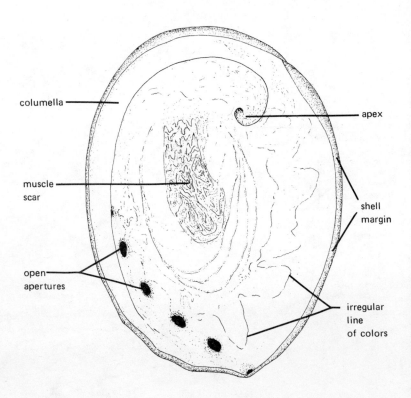

Usually flat, thin-shelled abalones are those which have grown swiftly.   Thick, highly arched shells represent older abalones that have not had optimum food and environmental conditions for growth. Shell injuries, caused by abalone irons and marauding crabs, also retard shell growth, at least until the damages mend. This results in a shelflike increment on the shell. Boring sponges and clams cause the abalone to spread nacreous layers inside its shell, preventing organisms from penetrating to the animal itself, but resulting in a thick shell. This often creates blister pearls inside the shell.

Occasionally an irritation develops around the gonad (sex organ). This may result in the formation of a hollow, horn- or tooth-shaped pearl which encloses the gonad.   Other pearls sometimes grow under the shell margin.   These crescent-shaped forms, called baroque pearls, can be several inches long. Also, small round pearls may develop in the viscera (internal organs). These range from pearly white to dull tan and from iridescent bluish green to jet black. Some grow as large as marbles.

Most pearls are found in older shells.   Since they are usually imperfect, the market for them is limited.   However, good ones are relatively rare and may command a respectable price.

ABALONE PEARLS   Tooth-shaped pearls are from gonad; large crescent-shaped pearl is from under the columella; and small pearls are from gut. *(Photo by Rick Terry, Brooks Institute)*

ANATOMY

The abalone is rather primitive. Its nervous system lacks a brain per se; instead it has a nerve center with nerve cords leading to ganglia (clusters of nerve cells). These control its movements.

Myopic eyes exist on two retractable eyestalks similar to those of the familiar garden snail. The eyes can discern only vague changes between light and dark. The epipodeum, a circular fringe of tentacles surrounding the foot, is thought to be light sensitive as well. Extensive nerve endings leading from the epipodeum to the nerve center certainly indicate that some sensory function exists, although the tentacles may only be sensitive to water movements or touch. Paired organs of smell are present at the gill entrance, although their effectiveness is not known.

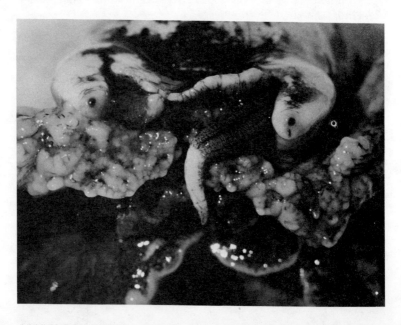

ABALONE'S FACE   This peculiar face, resembling that of a garden snail or slug, has myopic eyes on the ends of stalks, long feelerlike tentacles and a large cupped mouth. The tongue, often measuring one-third the animal's length, extrudes as the rasplike teeth (radula) are expended. *(Photo by Peter C. Howorth)*

The bulk of the animal consists of a huge muscular foot. The meat of the foot, including the muscle column attaching it to the shell, is used as food. Each legal-sized animal yields at least a quarter pound of meat; extremely large red abalones can yield as much as three pounds. The meat is nearly twenty-five percent protein and is low in fat.

Abalones are well-known for their incredible strength in clinging to rocks. The foot's tremendous surface area, which often equals the shell diameter, provides considerable surface adhesion. This huge suction cup, aided by water displacement and protected by a massive shield of shell, makes large abalones almost invulnerable.

Abalones are able to sense food at close ranges. Once a morsel is detected, the abalone will glide slowly along, feeling its way, until it reaches the alga. It then raises its foot, comes down on the plant and traps it. If disturbed while feeding, the abalone will quickly clamp down, pulling its shell over itself. In this position it is difficult, if not impossible, for most predators to remove it.

ANATOMY OF AN ABALONE

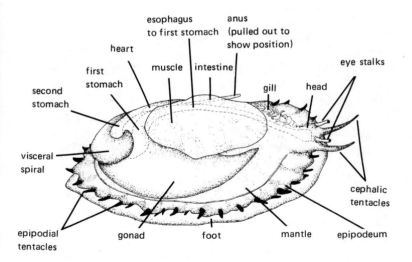

Once the alga is trapped, the abalone will begin devouring it by rasping off sections with its radula. This filelike tongue may equal nearly one-third the animal's length when fully extended, although most of the radula consists of developing teeth. Presumably the animal continually replaces the worn-out end of its tongue.

The food passes into the esophagus, where initial digestion occurs, then to the first of two stomachs. From the second stomach it passes through the intestine. Waste products are carried out the anus, a straw-like tube under the shell apertures.

An abalone's heart operates much the same as any invertebrate's, except that the intestine passes through one of the cavities. The blood is watery, with a slight bluish tint; as mentioned earlier, it has no coagulative qualities.

Abalones have gills located under the open row of apertures. The openings apparently allow a free exchange of water over the gills even when the animal is clamped tightly down. Waste products as well as gametes may also be passed through the apertures.

The gonad is a large horn-shaped organ under the epipodeum along the growing edge of the shell. The male abalone has a tan-colored gonad; the female, a green one.

NATURAL ENEMIES

Sea otters are the chief natural predators of abalones. Otters remove abalones by smashing the shells with rocks. Without shells, abalones are completely helpless. After abalones become scarce in an area, otters overturn rocks to find more. When there is practically nothing left, most otters will move to find better foraging elsewhere. Only abalones in deep crevices and under heavy boulders survive. Rocky areas without these configurations are completely ravaged by sea otters.

At present, the otter herd of less than two thousand animals consumes almost ten million pounds of raw shellfish a year, or two and a half tons for each mature otter. Contrast this with the 1977 commercial abalone catch of less than two million pounds. The sport catch was slightly more, but both catches were made outside the otters' range and represent legal size abalones. But the otter certainly cannot be blamed for its appetite, nor for competing with man for food. Man created the problem and must learn to live with the sea otter. Careful management could restore much of the lost balance.

Rock or cancer crabs are also heavy predators of abalones. These crabs abound in rocky coastal areas from the intertidal zone out to over a hundred feet down. They prey upon young abalones by catching the edges of the shells with their powerful pincers. This prevents abalones from clamping down. While the animals are exposed, crabs feed upon them. As abalones weaken, they release their hold upon the rocks. If abalones clamp down quickly enough, the shell margins will be chipped by the lower half of the crabs' pincers. Once abalones are clamped tightly to rocks, crabs cannot remove them unless the abalones are very small. Often abalones' shells exhibit paired chips which have been mended by the animal. Such notches represent past battles with cancer crabs.

Most bottom fish feed on abalone meat, although only a few are able to remove abalones. Sheephead undoubtedly are the most voracious natural abalone predators in southern California. They follow divers in droves, often brazenly darting into divers' baskets to steal abalones. Large numbers of sub-legal abalones are lost to sheephead by thoughtless persons who pick abalones before measuring them. When shorts are not properly replaced, they are quickly gobbled up. The only way to be certain of the abalone's safety is to guard it until it is clamped down and cannot be removed.

When divers are not present, sheepheads undoubtedly catch abalones as they rise to feed on algae. Once abalones are flipped over, they are completely vulnerable.

Bat rays have been observed eating abalones, although how they remove them is unknown. Probably they too must take them by surprise. Moray eels eat abalones, but they usually steal them from other fish and withdraw with them into their lairs.

Cabezons replace sheepheads as main fish predators of abalones north of Point Conception. These fish, with their huge, bulbous heads and enormous mouths, are able to swallow surprisingly large abalones. Octopi also prey upon abalones, either by yanking them off rocks or

(reportedly) by drilling a hole through their shells and injecting a para-
lyzing venom. Starfishes probably eat juvenile abalones, although they
seem to be unable or unwilling to attack larger specimens.

Sometimes encysting worms are found within the tissues of abalones. These worms are especially common in senile specimens or those
exposed to poor environmental conditions. Various mollusks (see THE
ABALONE SHELL) also may bore into the shells, but they generally
are stopped by built-up layers of nacre.

Boring sponges are probably the worst abalone parasites. They
bore hundreds of tiny holes into the shell, necessitating an extensive
build-up from inside to prevent holes from piercing the shell. Conse-
quently, all growing energies are spent thickening the shell rather than
enlarging it. The shell becomes porous and crumbly, offering scant
protection for the animal.

Commensal shrimps live just under abalone shells, but are not
parasitic. They may be found on the undersides of large sea urchins
as well.

COMPETITORS FOR THE SAME FOOD   This large red abalone, camouflaged
by algae growing on its shell, must move out when voracious sea urchins take
over its grazing area. (*Photo by Rick Terry, Brooks Institute*)

Sea urchins frequent areas adjacent to abalone beds. They move rapidly in large numbers, often stripping the bottom of algal growth. They are more voracious feeders than the rather sessile abalones. When an area has been denuded by extensive sea urchin grazing, abalones must move or face a greatly reduced food input. Abalones are occasionally outgrazed to starvation, since they move only when subjected to dire stress, and even then, not always.

Some abalones live in areas totally free of algal growth and yet are in excellent condition. Such areas are often natural collecting spots for drifting material. Rocks form water vortexes which collect algae torn loose by wave action.

From central California to Alaska, abalones frequently wash ashore during storms. Why they lose their holds on rocks is unknown. A direct physical battering from waves, coupled with crashing stones and debris, might weaken them so that they lose their grip. Excessive freshwater inundations may also kill them. Presumably winter storms affect only shallow abalone beds.

Considerable sand movements occur throughout the year. Although abalones have been observed living under a few inches of sand, extensive sand deposition often will bury them several feet deep. If the sand remains for long, abalones must move or perish.

Red tide, a "living soup" of microorganisms, also wipes out countless invertebrates. A sufficient concentration can burn up enough oxygen to suffocate abalones. This occurs occasionally along the Pacific coast.

COLOR PLATE I.   Red Abalone, *Haliotis rufescens*   *(Live photo by Rick Terry;*
shell photos by Dorothy Lawson, Brooks Institute)

50

COLOR PLATE II. Black Abalone, *Haliotis cracherodii* *(Live photo by Peter C. Howorth; shell photos by Dorothy Lawson, Brooks Institute)*

COLOR PLATE III. Corrugated or Pink Abalone, *Haliotis corrugata* (*Live photo by Peter C. Howorth; shell photos by Dorothy Lawson, Brooks Institute)*

COLOR PLATE IV. Green Abalone, *Haliotis fulgens* (*Live photo by Rick Terry; shell photos by Dorothy Lawson, Brooks Institute*)

COLOR PLATE V. Flat Abalone, *Haliotis walallensis* (Live photo by Peter C. Howorth; shell photos by Dorothy Lawson, Brooks Institute)

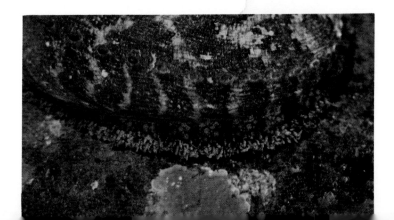

COLOR PLATE VI. White or Sorensen Abalone, *Haliotis sorenseni* (*Live photo by Peter C. Howorth; shell photos by Dorothy Lawson, Brooks Institute*)

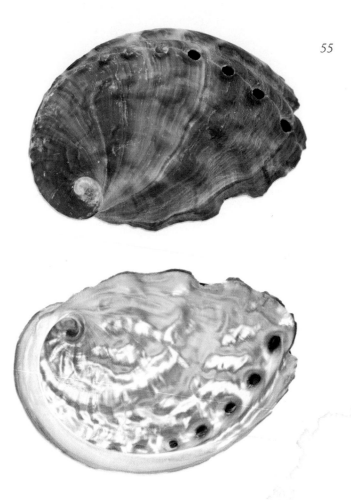

COLOR PLATE VII. Pinto Abalone, *Haliotis kamtschatkana kamtschatkana*
(Live photo by Peter C. Howorth; shell photos by Dorothy Lawson, Brooks
Institute)

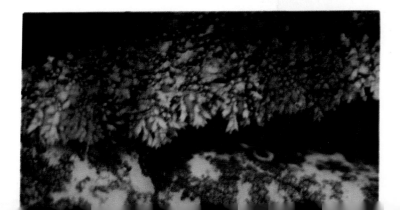

COLOR PLATE VIII. Threaded Abalone, *Haliotis kamtschatkana assimilis* (*Live photo by Peter C. Howorth; shell photos by Dorothy Lawson, Brooks Institute)*

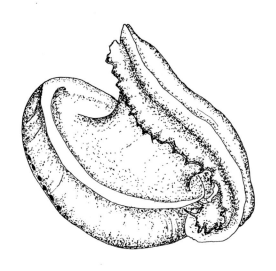

PART IV

AMERICAN ABALONE SPECIES

IDENTIFICATION

There are eight species and five subspecies of American abalones. Each is identifiable by particular characteristics. Since animals encountered in natural surroundings often have heavily encrusted shells, it is essential to be able to identify each species by characteristics of the animal alone.

Although animals vary little, shells vary tremendously. Some species have only one or two open holes, while others have four or five. Some have high, thick, wavy shells; some are thin and flat. A number have finely etched imbrications on the shell surfaces. Still others have been eroded by scouring sand and pebbles.

When identifying abalones, it is always best to rely upon several features rather than one key feature. Read the following descriptions carefully, for the photographs only illustrate typical forms, and variation is the rule rather than the exception in abalones. Never be misled by common names referring to coloration. Colors may not be visible, nor do they necessarily represent the abalone in question.

Six of the seven west coast abalones hybridize, producing beautiful variations. Hybrid identification should be left to experts, because hybrids are rarely encountered by most pickers.* *If there is ever any doubt as to the correct identification of an abalone, either leave it alone, or pick the largest size limit from all possibilities.*

RED ABALONE, *Haliotis rufescens* (Color Plate I, p. 49)

The red abalone is characterized by thick, jet-black tentacles. The epipodeum (the circular fringe of skin around the foot) is also black, occasionally with alternating gray stripes. The growing edge of the shell usually has a wide, bright red margin, although some specimens may have light pink, green or even white margins. The adult shell is quite large, sometimes being over eleven inches (28 cm). This is the largest of approximately one hundred abalone species found world-wide.

Slow-growing specimens, particularly along the coast, have thick, wavy shells lacking fine sculpturing. Fast-growing specimens have thin, flat shells etched with fine spiral lines that are parallel to the aperture row. There are three to five moderately elevated apertures, although older, thicker shells may have only one or two. The outsides are a dull brick red with concentric bands of pink or pale green. The apexes are often bright green, merging to red. This indicates the drastic dietary change which occurs when juveniles emerge from hiding and eat a different alga. The insides of these shells are multicolored, with iridescent green, pink, and copper predominating. A prominent muscle scar is present.

The red abalone ranges from southern Oregon to Baja California. In Southern California, below Point Conception, it is commonly found from twenty to one hundred feet down. At Catalina and San Clemente islands, and from Baja California to Malibu, it is usually found deeper than fifty or sixty feet. (It has been reported as deep as five hundred forty feet.) In San Luis Obispo County, the red abalone may be found out to one hundred feet or more, while farther north, all the way to southern Oregon, it occurs from the low tide zone out to about fifty feet.

* For more information on hybrids, see *Hybridization in the Eastern Pacific Abalones (Haliotis)*, by Buzz Owen, © 1971, Bulletin No. 9 of Los Angeles County Museum of Natural History.

This distribution by depth from one locale to the next reflects environmental differences. Red abalones prefer water from forty-five to approximately sixty degrees Fahrenheit. They prefer macro-algae as food, primarily giant kelp in the south and bull kelp in the north. In deep water they eat elk kelp. Red abalones also eat feather-boa and bladder chain kelp in shallow southern waters, and palm kelp in medium depths in Southern and Central California.

BLACK ABALONE, *Haliotis cracherodii* (Color Plate II, p. 50)

The black abalone is the only species which might be confused with a red abalone under water. Like the red, its tentacles and epipodeum are jet-black. The black abalone is usually much smaller than the red, however. The edge of the black abalone's shell is narrow and generally bluish or greenish black. Occasionally specimens are found with dull, orange-red shells which can be confused with small red abalones. There the similarity ends.

The black abalone shell is smooth and circular in outline, unlike the wavy, oval red abalone shell. It is pierced with five to nine apertures. Old, senile specimens may have fewer holes. (Some were once found with no holes and dubbed as subspecies *imperforata*. These have since been considered merely variations and not subspecies.) The outsides of black abalone shells usually are black, occasionally with orange-red concentric dietary banding (see THE ABALONE SHELL). They grow to over eight inches (20 cm), although the average is much smaller.

The inside of the black is silvery, with no muscle scar, although large, fast-growing specimens sometimes have tints of iridescent blue and green and a partially or completely developed muscle scar.

Blacks are the Bogarts of the abalone world. They usually inhabit surf-battered rocks from the low tide zone out to twelve or fifteen feet of water. In areas where the bottom slants sharply downward and little space is available, they may be found in deeper water. I found one living thirty-five feet down. A prominent scar etched into the rock it was clinging to indicated that it had been there some time.

Blacks live from Northern California to Baja. They are able to tolerate a range in water temperature from forty-five to seventy-five degrees Fahrenheit. Littoral black abalone beds are exposed to direct sunlight during low tides, which increases temperatures even more. They usually cling tightly to rocks while exposed and do not move about.

A subspecies is found at Guadalupe Island off Mexico (*Haliotis cracherodii californiensis*). This abalone is smaller, higher, and has twelve to sixteen apertures.

Black abalones prefer algae such as giant and feather-boa kelp. When hungry they will seize other algae which drift within their reach.

CORRUGATED OR PINK ABALONE, *Haliotis corrugata*
(Color Plate III, p. 51)

The corrugated abalone is easy to differentiate from others by its black tentacles and black and white, lacelike epipodeum. No others have these characteristics. The exposed shell edge, which is dark red to turquoise in color, is often corrugated like the core of a cardboard box.

The shell surface is also heavily corrugated. This can be masked by growths or eroded away. The shell is plump, circular, and usually has two or three highly elevated apertures which may be fluted in fast growing specimens. It grows to over eight inches (20 cm). The outside is dull brick red with turquoise banding. Occasionally, all-turquoise shells are found. These are valuable to collectors.

The inside boasts a large muscle scar and iridescent swirls of blue, green, pink and copper.

Corrugated abalones range from Jalama Beach, California, to Baja California and as far north as San Miguel Island. They are found from the intertidal zone out to nearly two hundred feet of water. A subspecies (*Haliotis corrugata oweni*) is found at Guadalupe Island.

These abalones feed mainly upon giant kelp, although they eat other algae in extremely shallow or deep water.

GREEN ABALONE, *Haliotis fulgens* (Color Plate IV, p. 52)

The green abalone (formerly called the blue abalone) may be

readily distinguished by its light green or gray tentacles. The epipodeum is mottled with either brown or olive-drab. The protruding edge of the shell is quite thin and usually reddish brown in color.

The shell surface is sculptured with evenly spaced, cordlike ridges paralleling the aperture row. The shell is oval and rather shallow, and the surface is woody brown or olive-green. A dark red band often connects the five to seven modestly elevated apertures that pierce the shell surface. As in other abalones, older, senile specimens may have fewer *open* holes. Greens may grow to over nine inches (23 cm). The inside of the shell is a striking fantasia of blue, copper and green iridescent patterns, including an extremely brilliant and beautiful muscle scar.

The green abalone ranges from Santa Barbara to Baja California. It exists on the Channel Islands as far up as Santa Rosa. A subspecies (*Haliotis fulgens quadalupensis*) is found at Guadalupe Island. The subspecies is smaller, but higher, and is sculptured with strong cording on the shell surface. This deep cording pattern may often be mirrored on the inside.

Greens prefer shallow water from the low tide zone out to twenty-five feet or so. In the south they are found out to sixty feet and more. The preferred diet is feather-boa and giant kelp, although smaller red algae may also be eaten.

FLAT ABALONE, *Haliotis walallensis* (Color Plate V, p. 53)

The flat abalone (formerly called the northern green abalone) is similar to the green abalone except that the tentacles are dark green or brown and quite long. The very delicate and frilly epipodeum is splotchy yellowish brown and light green. The exposed edge of shell usually is dark red or green.

The outside is very flat—hence the name—and ornamented with spiral cords of unequal thickness and spacing. Raised imbrications counter these cords, paralleling the growing edge. The shell is usually green and/or red, often with light oblique streaks. A dark red band may connect the aperture row. A series of whitish bands also extends from the apertures to the margin. These bands are particularly evident in juveniles. The shell is elongated and oval, and reaches a length of over five inches (13.5 cm).

The inside of the flat abalone shell is pearly white. In large specimens, nacreous clumps may exist where the muscle was attached.

Flat abalones are found from British Columbia to the Mexican border. Below Point Conception, California, they are rather rare and are seldom seen shallower than eighty feet. For this reason they cannot be confused with the green, a much shallower species. There is little or no overlap within the depth ranges of these two species. In Central California, flats are more abundant and are generally found from twenty to sixty feet down. Farther north they are found in protected crevices from the intertidal zone out to approximately fifty feet. This abalone is a cosmopolitan feeder and grazes on a variety of algae.

WHITE or SORENSEN ABALONE, *Haliotis sorenseni*
(Color Plate VI, p. 54)

The white abalone has yellowish tentacles, occasionally with greenish tints. The epipodeum is mottled with yellowish or brownish beige, while the foot often appears a striking bright orange. The exposed edge of the shell is usually quite thin, with red or pink predominating.

The shell is circular, highly-arched, rather plump and characteristically very thin. The color is dull, pale red, often with a bright orange apex. In twenty-five to fifty percent of white abalones, the apex has an orange band parallel to the aperture row. This band always fades into a uniform, pale red color by the time the shell reaches over two inches or so in length. The orange band remains near the apex, however. This unique characteristic enables researchers to easily distinguish white abalone hybrids from others because the orange band found in other hybrids continues throughout the entire shell, whereas in the white it fades out.

White abalones sometimes hybridize with reds. Virtually thousands of these hybrids have been found, although the next most common hybrid numbers less than a hundred out of literally millions of shells examined.

White abalone shells are characterized by gently etched, regular spiral lines. They generally have three to five well-elevated apertures and reach nearly nine inches (22.5 cm) in length.

The insides are consistently pearly white, with no muscle scar except for occasional nacreous clumps in large specimens.

White abalones occur sporadically from Point Conception, California, to Baja California. They range as far north as San Miguel Island. (A few are reportedly found in very deep water off Guadalupe Island, although these have not received a subspecies designation as yet.) White abalones are usually found from thirty-five to over one hundred feet down. They definitely have a preference for deep water, feeding on elk kelp and giant kelp, together with various smaller algae when nothing else is available.

PINTO ABALONE, *Haliotis kamtschatkana kamtschatkana*
(Color Plate VII, p. 55)

The pinto abalone is characterized by light yellowish-brown tentacles (sometimes green in the northern states) and a mottled pale yellow and dark brown epipodeum. Often the fringes are tinted with orange. The edge of the shell may be almost any color, but most typically is either pale red or green.

This animal may be distinguished from the other subspecies (*Haliotis kamtschatkana assimilis*) by the nearly straight growing edge of the shell, a characteristic unique to this subspecies. Also, the shell surface is lumpy compared with its smooth southern counterpart.

The roughly oval shell is adorned with numerous threadlike spiral cords alternating with narrow spiral lines. Colors range from reddish brown to pale orange, usually with blue and/or green oblique streaks and/or chevron markings. Juveniles frequently have oblique white bands extending from the shell edge to the apertures. A dark red line sometimes connects the apertures. Color patterns may vary considerably (see also description of threaded abalone), but this is the most typical form. The shell reaches five inches (12.5 cm) or more in length and usually has from four to six open holes.

The inside of the shell is an iridescent pearly white, with the outside lumps mirrored on the inside. On large specimens, nacreous clusters or partially defined muscle scars are sometimes present.

Pinto abalones are found from the Aleutians to Point Conception, California. From Washington north, they may be found intertidally, although in the south they are generally found from twenty to fifty feet down. Their diet is considerably varied, evidenced by the many shell colors. They generally feed upon smaller algae.

The pinto abalone was formerly listed as a separate species (*Haliotis kamtschatkana*). Recent research resulted in the renaming of this species as a subspecies (*Haliotis kamtschatkana kamtschatkana*). In reality the two subspecies are simply regional variations of the same species. Supposedly the northern form will eventually revert to the southern form if transplanted (and vice versa).

THREADED ABALONE, *Haliotis kamtschatkana assimilis*
(Color Plate VIII, p. 56)

The threaded abalone animal looks the same as the pinto, although I have never observed one with green tentacles. (They are always yellowish brown or tan.) Because this animal is usually found from San Luis Obispo County south, it is seldom confused with the pinto, its northern counterpart.

The chief difference between these two subspecies lies in the appearances of the shells. The growing edge of the pinto is straight, or nearly so, whereas the growing edge of the threaded is round. The edge is visible underwater and may be used as one feature to identify this subspecies. Also, the surface of the threaded abalone is not lumpy as it is in the pinto. Four to six apertures are present, and the shell can grow to seven inches (18 cm) in exceptional cases.

The color of the threaded abalone probably varies more than any abalone species in the world. Specimens range from nearly white to pink; pale orange to red; red to dark brown. They also vary from light green to turquoise; from turquoise to dark green—and any combination of all these colors mentioned. The most typical is dark turquoise with light streaks and chevron marks on the shell surface. Usually a red streak connects the apertures, from which oblique, whitish bands radiate toward the shell margin.

A rare color form occurs in five to ten percent of the threaded abalones found. This consists of a spiral, bright orange band originating at the apex and continuing to the growing edge. The band contrasts vividly with the rest of the shell, creating a remarkably beautiful form of considerable value to shell collectors.

The threaded abalone shell is sculptured with numerous, thread-like spiral cords which give this abalone its name. The inside, like the pinto, is pearly white, although it is comparatively smooth and un-rippled. Nacreous welts may be present where the muscle was attached.

Threaded abalones range from Central to Baja California, usually from thirty to over one hundred feet down. Their highly varied diet is emphasized by the incredible variety of colors on the shells.

FLORIDA or POURTALES ABALONE, *Haliotis pourtalesii*

The Florida abalone is the only abalone found on the east coast. It is extremely rare, for only a few specimens have been found. All have been recovered off the Florida coast from dredging operations conducted in three hundred fifty to twelve hundred feet of water.

This abalone is approximately an inch (2.5 cm) in length. The oval, rather flat shell is sculptured with twenty-two to twenty-seven spiral cords. The outside is pale yellow or tan with darker splotches. Light orange bands extend from each aperture to the shell margin. The inside of the shell is pearly white. I have been unable to find any description of the animal.

Shell collectors should be very careful when purchasing specimens of the Florida abalone because unscrupulous dealers have been known to sell juvenile forms of foreign abalones as this species. Be certain each Florida abalone shell offered matches the description and photo in this text.

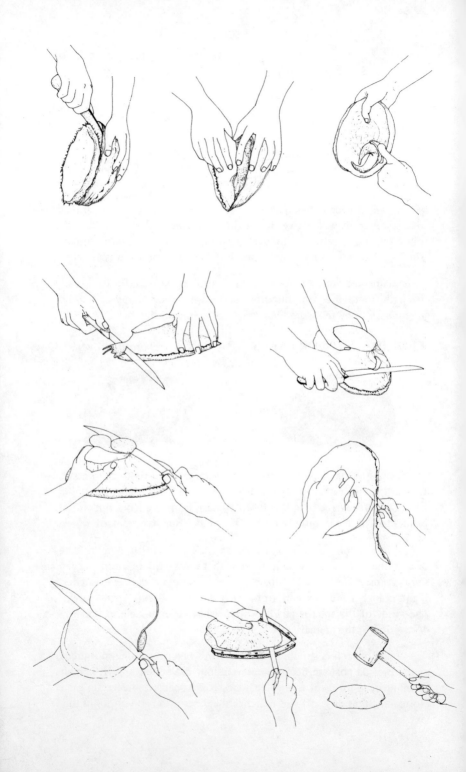

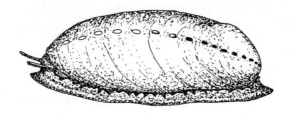

PART V

PREPARING ABALONES

CLEANING

The first step in cleaning an abalone is to remove the animal from its shell. Place the shell, apex down, on a hard surface. Insert an abalone iron or "shucking bar" under the meat close to the aperture row and near the growing edge. Jam the iron forcefully downward inside the shell, which will pop the muscle loose. With practice this can be done without damaging the meat.

Next, flip the shell over, so the end with the apertures is facing down. Using the web of each hand, separate the gut from the meat by spreading your hands in opposite directions. Flip the gut out of the shell with your forefinger. *Since the shells often have sharp edges, it is wise to wear gloves.*

The gut may be discarded or saved for fish bait. The shell should be placed outdoors, with the inside facing away from the sun.

Next, thoroughly wash the abalone. This is done by machines

in commercial processing shops. It is important to wash it well, since sand and other debris will dull cutting tools. Remove the head by lifting it back and cutting upward. The head can join the gut in the garbage or bait bucket.

The next stage is simple. Let the muscle relax on a flat, cool, shaded surface. Some abalones, such as whites and pinks, only need to flatten for an hour or two. Reds and blacks may take up to a day if the weather is cold.

Next is "up trimming." Place the abalone heel down like an inverted mushroom on the table, and cut away the tough skin from bottom to top. If the muscle is bumpy, discolored and tough where it was attached to the shell, skin it also. This is called a "cap cut" by processors. The best abalone trimming knives have ten-inch blades about five-eighths of an inch wide. They are stainless steel, hollow-ground and quite flexible.

Next, remove the epipodeum. This is called "edge trimming" in the shops and is usually done with a modified slicing machine. For home processing, cut off the epipodeum with a knife. Trim the black skin off so that a circular white collar of meat is exposed around the foot. Trim only far enough to reach the white part, which is fine, usable meat.

The next step is to remove the heel or foot. Cut away the skin until only the meat is showing. Known as "heel cutting," this process is also done by machine in the shops. Test the meat by driving your fingernail into it. If it is difficult to pierce, cut off a little more until your nail easily penetrates it.

The final cleaning stage, called "finish" or "clean-up trim," is to remove any last pieces of skin. Save the trimmings from each stage. They can be used later.

Slicing is next. Done by machines in processing shops, it may be done at home with a simple cutting board. Break a wooden coat hanger in half in the center and nail it in the shape of a "V" to a board. Wedge your trimmed abalone into the "V" and slice it. The coat hanger serves as a thickness guide while you slice the steaks.

The last step is pounding to tenderize the tough meat. Use a flat, immovable surface. Be certain the steaks and the pounding surface are relatively dry, otherwise the steaks will fly off when struck.

Thoroughly pound each steak until it is completely tenderized. Any meat tenderizing mallet will do, although enormous hardwood mallets are used in the shops. Try to avoid digging into the steaks with the edges of the mallet as this will break them. Hit them flat.

Pound the heel cut, or bottom slice, on the tough side. The same applies to the cap cut (where the muscle was attached to the shell).

The steaks should be eaten quickly or frozen. Freeze steaks in small sandwich bags, one for each steak. Place them on a flat tray so they may be stacked after they are frozen. When they are in individual bags, each steak may be easily separated for immediate defrosting and cooking.

If a meat grinder is available, grind up the trimmings as finely as possible for use as patties. If no grinder is available, trim can be frozen and used later to garnish rice (see RECIPES). It may also be used as bait.

RECIPES

"Pop" Ernest Doelter's Original Abalone Recipe

1 pound sliced, tenderized abalone steaks	1 beaten egg
	3 tablespoons dry sherry
1 teaspoon freshly ground pepper	½ cube of butter

"Slices of the meat placed on a hard surface are pounded with a heavy wooden mallet or rolling pin to break the tissue. Without a properly spirited pounding, the abalone is too tough to eat, but, if assaulted too savagely, it becomes mush. The slices are dipped in beaten egg thinned with dry sherry, then fried in butter in a heavy skillet, one minute to a side." *Serves two to four people.*

Fried Abalone Steaks

1 pound sliced, tenderized
    abalone steaks

1 beaten egg

½ cup cracker or bread crumbs

½ cube butter

1 lemon, sliced into wedges

1 fresh parsley sprig
    (optional)

This is the most popular recipe. Pour crumbs into plastic or paper bag. Dip each steak into beaten egg, then drop into bag and shake until coated with crumbs. Quick-fry in melted butter over medium hot flame, half a minute to a minute each side, or until golden brown. Serve with lemon wedges and parsley, salt and pepper to taste. Unthinned cream of mushroom soup, spiced with a dash of hot sauce and one minced garlic clove, can be added as gravy. *Enough for two to four people.*

Fire-Baked Abalones

4 whole abalones in shells   ½ cup soy sauce

Build a large wood fire on the beach in a rock-lined pit or in a barbecue. Wait until the fire has burned to flaming, red-hot coals, then throw in whole abalones in shells. Test shells periodically with poker: when they crumble away from meat, remove them from fire. This usually takes forty-five minutes to an hour. Cut away charred portions of meat, then slice remainder into bite-sized chunks. Dip in soy sauce and eat on the spot. *Serves four to six people.*

Abalone Jerky

1 whole, trimmed abalone

4 beef or chicken bouillon
    cubes

2 teaspoons freshly ground
    pepper

8 tablespoons salt or 2 quarts
    salt water

Immerse abalone in pot filled with salt water. Add four bouillon cubes and pepper, then boil for one hour. Cut meat into thin strips. To dry, put in oven rack at lowest heat overnight or until strips are thoroughly dry, or else wrap in cheesecloth and dry for at least one week in hot sun. One abalone will make about twelve strips of jerky.

Abalone Burgers

1 pound finely ground abalone trim

2 cups bread crumbs

1 egg

1 chopped bell pepper

1 chopped onion

4 chopped celery stalks

½ cube butter

½ pound sliced mild cheese (optional)

6 onion rolls

Mayonnaise, lettuce, sliced tomatoes, ketchup, mustard

Thoroughly wash one pound of abalone trim. If possible, spray it with a garden hose nozzle while holding it in a sieve. This will remove much of the dark pigment on the skin. Grind trim as finely as possible, preferably in an electric food grinder. Repeat, then mix trim with bread crumbs, egg, bell pepper, onion and celery. Form into six half-inch-thick patties, then quick-fry in butter until golden brown. Melt sliced cheese over patties if desired. Next, make into six hearty burgers, using mayonnaise, lettuce, tomatoes, ketchup and mustard as preferred. Salt and pepper to taste. *Serves four to six people.*

Abalone Slivers and Rice

½ pound "up trim" or "cap cuts" (see CLEANING)

1 cup water

½ cube butter

¼ cup soy sauce

2 quarts rice (cooked)

Thoroughly wash trim, then pressure cook in water for exactly seven minutes. Cool cooker immediately, remove the trim and drain. Sauté pieces lightly in butter, then serve over cooked rice of your choice with soy sauce as seasoning. Small pounded fragments of steaks may be substituted for trim if no pressure cooker is available. *This recipe makes plenty for four to six people.*

Avocado Abalone

2 small cans green chili peppers

½ pound Monterey jack cheese

1 pound sliced, tenderized abalone steaks

1 beaten egg

1 whole avocado   ½ cup cracker or bread crumbs

Dip steaks in beaten egg, then shake in bag full of cracker crumbs. Finely slice peppers, Monterey jack cheese and avocado. Lay ingredients on abalone steak, roll steak up tightly and secure in place with toothpick. Bake in uncovered casserole dish fifteen minutes at three hundred fifty degrees. Absolutely delicious. *Serves two to four people.*

Abalone Mexicana is another variation of this recipe. Stuff and roll steaks as above, then quick-fry in butter until golden brown. Place steaks in casserole dish and add a small can of tomato paste, one freshly minced garlic clove, and a quarter of an onion, finely chopped. Cover with half a cup grated Monterey jack cheese and bake at three hundred seventy-five degrees until cheese has melted. Excellent with fried rice. *Helpings for two to four people.*

Abalone Fondue

1 pound sliced, tenderized   1 cup cooking oil
   abalone steaks

Cut tenderized steaks into cubes. Drop into hot oil in fondue dish and simmer until done. This usually takes about one minute. Serve with lemon wedges, soy sauce or tartar sauce according to individual preference. Excellent as *hors d'oeuvres*. *Serves two to four people.*

Baked Abalone a la Martin

1 trimmed, not sliced, whole red   1 teaspoon salt
   abalone or
                                       1 teaspoon pepper
2 trimmed, not sliced, whole
   pink abalones   ½ cup dry white wine

                                       ½ cup water
½ cup cooking oil
                                       1 freshly minced garlic clove
½ cup flour
                                       1 teaspoon cornstarch

Carefully and thoroughly pound all surfaces of abalone, retaining its upside-down mushroom shape. Smear with oil, then sprinkle on flour, salt and pepper. Brown lightly in frying pan, then place in casserole dish. Add wine, water and minced garlic clove, then cover and bake for thirty to forty minutes at three hundred seventy-five degrees. Slice diagonally into three or four pieces before serving. Juice may be thickened with cornstarch if gravy is desired. *Feeds two to four persons.*

Abalone Chowder

1 pound sliced, tenderized abalone steaks	4 cups milk
2 cups water	½ cube butter
6 slices bacon	1 teaspoon salt
1 large, chopped onion	1 teaspoon pepper
6 chopped celery stalks	1 teaspoon cornstarch (optional)
4 cups cubed potatoes	6 saltines or 12 oyster crackers (optional)

Dice abalone steaks into cubes, add to potatoes and let simmer in pot with water. Fry bacon until crisp, drain and set aside. In the bacon fat, cook onion and celery until nearly done. Pieces should be slightly crunchy. Drain and add vegetables and butter to abalone and potatoes. Simmer very slowly, adding a cup of milk every five minutes. Salt and pepper to taste, and add cornstarch if thicker chowder is desired. Crackers may be included according to individual preference. When last cup of milk has been added, break bacon into bits and add to pot. Allow pot to barely simmer for an additional fifteen minutes, then serve. A nice touch is to serve this in abalone shells which have had the holes sealed with epoxy (see CLEANING SHELLS). Mussel shells make attractive spoons. *Enough for six or eight people.*

CLEANING SHELLS

The first step is simply to be selective. Pick shells with little or no growth, unchipped margins and healthy surfaces. Shells riddled with holes are poor specimens.

Place shells in a remote corner of your backyard, insides facing down, for two weeks or more. The growths dry up and become brittle, making them easier to remove. Anthills are excellent spots for shells. The ants will industriously clean out much of the remaining animal material.

Scrub the surface of each shell with a stiff wire brush. Brush parallel to the lines on the shell surface. A wire wheel may also be used, but be certain to wear eye protection and a protective mask. Provide plenty of ventilation, since the fine dust from the cleaning is poisonous and can cause silicosis of the lungs.

Remove stubborn growths, such as barnacles, with a small chisel. Once the shell is clean, coat the inside with mineral oil, vaseline or silicone spray. This protects the delicate pigments inside. Submerge the shell in straight bleach and leave it in for approximately half an hour.

Check the shell periodically until it is cleaned to your satisfaction. This may take up to a day for some. Next, the shell should be thoroughly washed, dried, and then coated with mineral oil, which will soak into the surface and impart a lifelike luster. Resins, shellacs, varnishes and the like are frowned upon by shell buffs, since they yellow and crack with age. They also impart an unnatural sheen to the shells.

Acids may be used topically to remove stubborn stains and growths. However, too much acid will destroy the delicate shell sculpturing and eventually eat through to the nacreous inner layer.

The shells should be displayed indoors and kept out of the sunlight, because they will fade if exposed too long. Shells dulled with age can be rinsed, scrubbed, then plunged into acid for a few seconds to brighten them up. Mineral oil can be added to restore the sheen. Carefully preserved shells will last a lifetime, serving as a constant reminder of this great gastropod that has delighted so many people.

APPENDIXES

SYSTEMATIC POSITION OF AMERICAN ABALONES

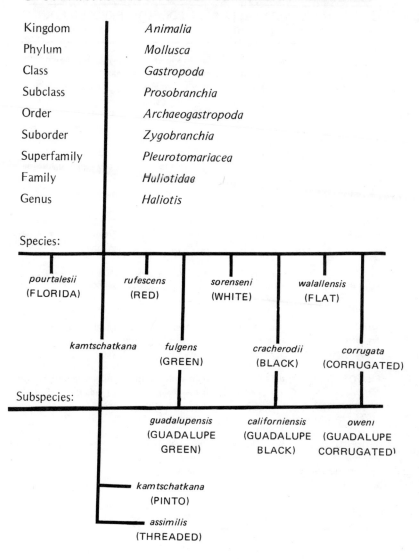

Kingdom	*Animalia*
Phylum	*Mollusca*
Class	*Gastropoda*
Subclass	*Prosobranchia*
Order	*Archaeogastropoda*
Suborder	*Zygobranchia*
Superfamily	*Pleurotomariacea*
Family	*Haliotidae*
Genus	*Haliotis*

Species:

pourtalesii
(FLORIDA)

rufescens
(RED)

sorenseni
(WHITE)

walallensis
(FLAT)

kamtschatkana

fulgens
(GREEN)

cracherodii
(BLACK)

corrugata
(CORRUGATED)

Subspecies:

guadalupensis
(GUADALUPE
GREEN)

californiensis
(GUADALUPE
BLACK)

oweni
(GUADALUPE
CORRUGATED)

kamtschatkana
(PINTO)

assimilis
(THREADED)

KEY TO IDENTIFYING PACIFIC ABALONES UNDER WATER*

SPECIES	TENTACLE COLOR	EPIPODEUM	EXPOSED EDGE OF SHELL
RED *Haliotis rufescens*	black, some- times with gray ones also	black, sometimes with evenly spaced gray or tan stripes	wide, red margin, gently wavy
BLACK *Haliotis cracherodii*	black	black or gray	round, black margin, sometimes dull orange
CORRUGATED *Haliotis corrugata*	black	appears black & white, lacelike under water	corrugated; light blue or dull red, sometimes both
GREEN *Haliotis fulgens*	light green or gray	olive-drab or brown, mottled & frilly	thin, rippled, dark green or reddish brown margin
FLAT *Haliotis walallensis*	dark green or brown	light, splotched with brown & yellow; lacelike	thin, even; green or dark red
WHITE *Haliotis sorenseni*	light greenish yellow	mottled brown & yellow, often with orange foot	gently wavy or round; very thin, dull brick red
PINTO *Haliotis kamtschatkana kamtschatkana*	tan or beige	light yellow with brown splotches, edges sometimes orange	usually reddish brown or green; straight but wavy
THREADED *Haliotis kamtschatkana assimilis*	tan or beige	light yellow with brown splotches, edges sometimes orange	almost any combination of colors; round & even

* These keys (also p. 77) are based upon the most frequently observed forms; for a detailed description of each species, refer to PART IV.

KEY TO IDENTIFYING PACIFIC ABALONE SHELLS

SPECIES	SHELLS	COLOR	INSIDE	FEATURES
RED *Haliotis rufescens*	oval, wavy, 3 to 5 holes	brick red; sometimes with light blue or green banding	multicolored, iridescent, large muscle scar	massive size
BLACK *Haliotis cracherodii*	smooth, circular, 5-9 holes flush with surface	bluish black, some with dull orange concentric banding	pearly white, no scar except in very large ones	smooth, black shell
CORRUGATED *Haliotis corrugata*	corrugated, circular, 2-3 holes	dull red and/ or turquoise	multicolored, iridescent, large muscle scar	corrugated shell
GREEN *Haliotis fulgens*	oval, flat, broad spiral cords, 5-7 holes	reddish brown and/or bluish green	multicolored, iridescent, large muscle scar	flatter than other common species, blue-green interior
FLAT *Haliotis walallensis*	oval, very flat, spiral cords with opp. ridges, 5-6 holes	dark red and/ or green with lighter streaks	pearly white, no muscle scar*	extremely flat, usually small
WHITE *Haliotis sorenseni*	round, fine spiral lines, 3-5 holes	dull brick red	pearly white, no muscle scar*	very thin, highly arched shell
PINTO *Haliotis kamtschatkana kamtschatkana*	lumpy, long, groove below holes; 4-6 holes	many colors; often reddish brown	pearly white, no muscle scar*	growing edge nearly straight line from apex to holes
THREADED *Haliotis kamtschatkana assimilis*	round, threadlike spiral lines, 4-6 holes	many colors; most typical dark turquoise with streaks of other colors	pearly white, no muscle scar*	threadlike spiral lines

* Nacreous clumps may be present where muscle was attached to shell.

RECOMMENDED BIBLIOGRAPHY

Bonnot. Paul. 1948. *The Abalones of California.* California Department of Fish and Game, Sacramento, CA.

Cox, Keith W. 1962. *California Abalones, Family Haliotidae.* California Department of Fish and Game, Sacramento, CA.

Morris, Percy A. 1966. *A Field Guide to Shells of the Pacific Coast and Hawaii.* Houghton Mifflin Company, Boston, MA.

Owen, Buzz. 1971. *Hybridization in the Eastern Pacific Abalones (Haliotis).* Bulletin Number 9 of Los Angeles County Museum of Natural History, Los Angeles, CA.

INDEX